St. Paul Street Provocations

by
Patti Ross

YELLOW ARROW
PUBLISHING
Baltimore, Maryland, USA

St. Paul Street Provocations
Copyright © 2021 by Yellow Arrow Publishing
All rights reserved.

ISBN (paperback) 978-1-7350230-6-9

Cover art of the mural "Walk the Line" from Baltimore-based muralists Jessie Unterhalter and Katey Truhn (jessieandkatey.com); photographed by Duane Winfield (duanewinfield.com). Interior artwork by Patti Ross.

Cover and interior design by Yellow Arrow Publishing.
For more information, see yellowarrowpublishing.com.

Table of Contents

Dedication	1
Bridge Over Two Blocks	5
Indemnity	7
The Deposer	9
Home/Less	11
Those Boys	13
Ghosting	17
A Letter to George Perry Floyd in Heaven	19
American Pie	21
History Month	27
About the Author	31

To my friends on the streets of Baltimore, Maryland. May you find peace in your journey. Thank you for being a part of mine.

With poetic love ~

Patti aka little pi 🖤

ST. PAUL STREET PROVOCATIONS

Bridge Over Two Blocks

Warning what you are about to hear may burn your ear off.
Warning these streets at night are not the place to be dropped off.
Warning Stefan was in that very spot when he got knocked off.
Warning the shit that happens on that street that neighborhood
        that city can make you want to
jump off the bridge.
Last week Marcia actually did.

Warning the bridge is very high.
Warning if you jump you will not survive.
Warning that block is rough.
Warning you will not survive.
Warning Pookie from across the bridge
        came across the bridge to that block.
Warning he got his ear cut off.
Warning he tried again.
Warning he got bumped off.
Warning this street ain't that block.

Or is it?

Indemnity

It took Colin Kaepernick to take a knee for you
        to pay attention to me.
Not because my brothers were getting killed.
Because it was on TV?
I thought you were kidding me.

A football game is worth more than a Black life?
Even after struggles and strife
        from roots of slavery and marginal lives?
Oh, right—it wasn't you.
        It was your ancestors who started the fight.
Don't you see the need to make right?

Why can't you see the boarded-up houses
                where I lay my head?
Homeless soldiers lay in the street dead.

Big Mama paid rent for decades,
        putting pretty flowers on her stoop.
She tried hard to change the neighborhood troop.
Told me it was a "nice white man"
        she gave her life's money too.
But, when she died, he left her treasures
        on the curb for looters to go through.
How am I supposed to believe he has compassion for me?

Stop coming at me with your "ifs" and "buts";
I've had enough.
        Time to move loud, proud, and fearless,
Truly make America great.
        I know the battle won't be tearless.

Look at me. I'm all American.
See the hue of my skin.
    Not African, not European—nothing but Dixie plantation.

When brothers take a knee,
    it has little to do with distant wars or fake treaties.
It is about what's happening to people in this country
    that look like me and the shitty way we are being treated.

America great again? What a joke; just ask Big Mama's folk.
A pickup truck came yesterday,
    loaded up what was left of her stay.
Threw it all in the back, just like trash on garbage day.

Now, I crossed the street and took a knee.
    Prayed for Big Mama, you, and me.
When my eyes opened from asking for PEACE,
I saw Big Mama's picture laying face up in the street.

Now, that "nice white man" said "get from HIS stoop."
As he put that 'For Rent' sign over my head,
I stood there for a minute wondering.
You think he gives a damn
    Big Mama is dead?

The Deposer

I was raped 36 years ago.
It is not on tape, no.
I do not want to remember,
But my limbs still go limp
When I hear that voice
That "yes" to my "no."

My pleas went to deaf ears as
I lay there in tears stolen,
My girlish charm realizing
I could be harmed by a boy
I said no to. I said no!
Yeah, it happened to me, too.

I tried deep inside to
Hide what had happened
I did not want to relive that.
It was hard enough to remember alone
Now the whole world would know.

My limbs still go limp when
I hear that voice that said "yes" to my "no."
He said yes; I said no.

I am standing here in tears
Realizing my greatest fear:
That my pleas land on deaf ears.
I was raped 36 years ago.

It is not on tape. No!

---

* Dedicated to Christine Margaret Blasey Ford, Professor at Stanford University who testified against Brett Michael Kavanaugh, Associate Justice of the Supreme Court of the United States.

Home/Less

> "The poor and the oppressor have this in common:
> The LORD gives sight to the eyes of both." Proverbs 29:13

Somebody asked me, "Why are you here?"
Let me be clear.
I am here for those who could not be here.
Who should be here but are consumed by fear,
lack of ear or dumb luck.
I am here for those riding high or ready to die.
I am standing for the man or the woman,
who sits on the side of society's lines.
Hides daily or rides in the back of
the Streetcar Named Desire.
They did not get hired or they just got fired.
Soon the times got tough, and they got roughed up.
Getting older on the streets, gets colder.
Now, nowhere to lay their head until they are dead.
Then, the city will reclaim them and put them in a plot of land
they might have had all along.
Might things have changed from the chains
    and the demons that reign.
Had they had that little plot or a dirt lot to call their own,
    to make a home.

Instead, they remained homeless.

Now, we are about the business of making money,
keeping our minds on it and ignoring the bodies piling up
on the streets that we drive, and the park benches we sit.
We know all the Hymns and the fake Tim's,
while ignoring those on the street dying and losing limbs.
Yeah, somebody asked me why am I here?
I am here for those that live with the demons of street life,
not knowing whether they get beat down tonight and

  die in the glow of a homeless light.

Why are you here?

---

* This is dedicated to "D" who lives at the corner of MLK and Fayette Street most nights. I wrote this after we talked one morning on my drive to work. The next day, I attended a neighborhood watch meeting.

Those Boys

The two of them look just alike.
Interesting how they fight.
Fists held up as if in flight.
Neither tries to flee.

Much too young to have this battle,
here on the city street. Why are they not
in the play yard where young children go to meet.

The asphalt that surrounds them,
telling a crumbled story of life.
Dirt path walkways make one wonder:
Will these boys survive?

Shoes untied and rocks in hand
the sound of their mother's ardent wrath.
One's nose is bloody; now the other's eye has swelled.
Others gather round the duo and end the fighting spell.

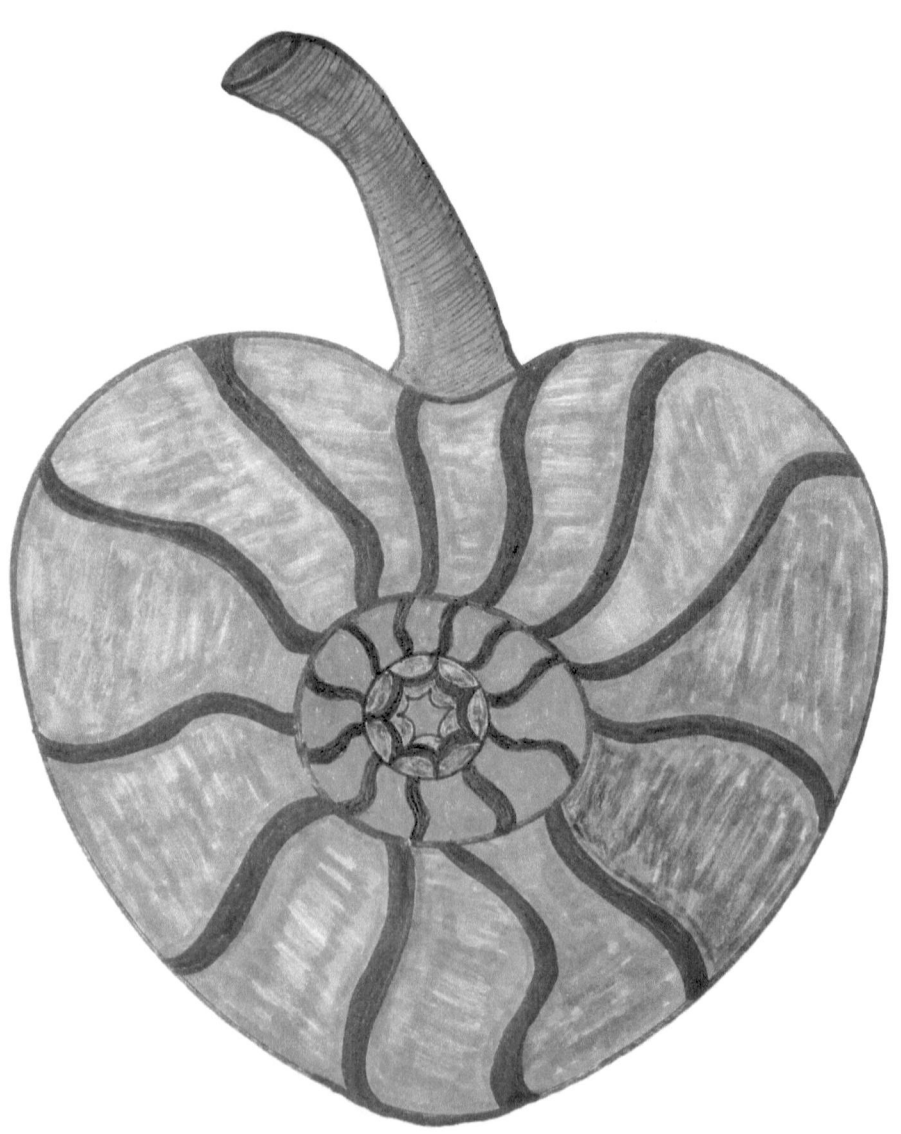

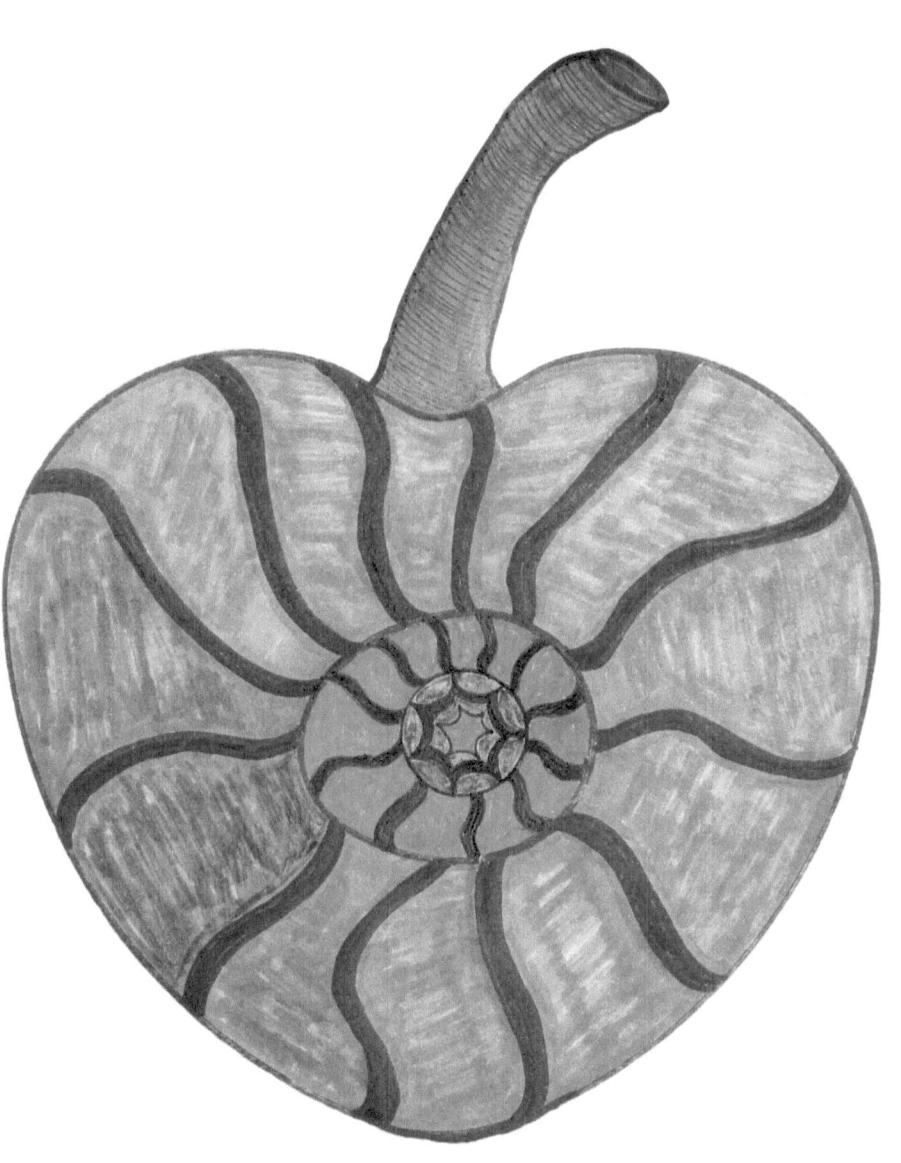

Ghosting

She looked at me without a flicker of recognition.
Her mother, my mother's sister.
I loved her.

We drank lemonade from grandmother's mason jars.
My brown skin glistened in the moonlight,
Her golden braids stretched across the back porch floor.

We counted stars.
She was with me in third grade and the same class in ninth.
At graduation that May we wore white.

It has been 10 years
Since Aunt Tee died.
I was there; she was not.

I saw her once in Baltimore.
A brief chat.
She had to go.

I never saw her again until today.
Summer in South Philadelphia is always hot.
The sun's beams sometimes make it hard to see.

I wanted to see her eyes smile.
She looked at me
Without a flicker of recognition.

A Letter to George Perry Floyd in Heaven

> "Do all these evildoers know nothing?
>
> They devour my people as though eating bread;
> they never call on the Lord.
> But there they are, overwhelmed with dread,
> for God is present in the company of the righteous.
> You evildoers frustrate the plans of the poor,
> but the Lord is their refuge."
> Psalm 14:4–6 NIV

Dear George,

Remember when you were a kid and
your mom like my mom told you the police were our friends.

Remember when you played cops and robbers.
Were you like me and always wanted to be the cop?
Because the police were good, and the robbers were bad.

George, do you remember when your friends
like my friends would get a spanking and
cry real hard and the spanking would stop.

Do you remember when you caught
the winning football pass and the crowd all cheered.

Do you remember when you cried for your mama
when she died and when you cried for her again and
she came and walked you to heaven.

I don't want you to remember the knee on your neck
or the one on your legs.
I will remember for you.

I will remember you.
I will pray you can breathe now.
I will remember that you could not
I will not let time forget.

American Pie

Billy Collins, former Poet Laureate (2001–2003), once said, "Poets spend a lot of time staring off in space." So I did, and with the song "American Pie" running in the background, I thought of this . . .

as I stare off in space
contemplating the place
which my race will end

up from the bottom
up from the ground
up from the worn soles
no bootstraps to hold

yes the story is getting old
sold to you a long
long time ago
not so

you see repercussions prevail and
reparations talk becomes a game
involving someone being shamed

politicians hold the reins
but remain uninterested
as they continue to get paid

yet we stand where
we stood 400 years ago
in the woods except now
it is called the Hood

that old man is not
running the plantation
no more now
he is running gentrification

while we were trying to catch up
on having a few things we missed the
bell that rings on Wall Street

we were busy straining
to find something to eat
well that old man
he is eating prime beef
just handed us a subprime lease

robbed of a piece of the American Pie
we are left with a black eye
folks pretend not to see
say they do not believe

blame the victim
that is always easy
a Narcissist leads
and the people bleed

American Pie
a song on how to die
for the privileged white boy
when the rainbow wasn't enuf

looking off in space
contemplating the place
where my race will end up
I will hold my head up

I know that
like cockroaches and flies
all of us won't die

so damn the whiskey and rye
damn the American Pie

History Month

Why my History got to be only one month long?

Didn't we suck from the same breast and sing the same songs?
We were both in that wash bucket.
Your dirt and mine intertwined,

Said we was brothers 'til Masa said "No!"
I am in the fields trying to forget that you
Lay's your head on my momma's lap.

Why my History got to be only one month long?

Isn't there a lot to tell from the 400 years
        riding the prairie alongside you?
Crispus took the first bullet for our flag so you leave me confused.
How can I not be patriotic? That is the thinking of those psychotic.

My ancestors' bones are the sand you sink your feet in at the beach.
Gazing across the water at their last loving memory.
One month of history?
        Their story is too long and too strong for that.

Why my History got to be only one month long?

Even though we pray to the same God.
How did he give you privilege and turn his back on me?
Was it when you made me
  "Black" and hang from the poplar tree?

Was it the week you burned down Tulsa
        making black Wall Street subprime?
Was it the day we started school, your old books now mine?
Was it the day they closed the Library because I was in line?

Why my History got to be only one month long?

You planning to shoot me in the back 16 times again.
Or leave me out of the game to die on the sidelines.
28 days is not enough time
        to explain the pain of living invisible and
being called out your name.

28 days is not enough time
        to explain why your mammie,
My mama got the same man.
It is too short of time to explain
That this land is my land built by "Black" hands.

Why my History got to be only one month long?

Is it because when the caged bird sings her song?
The shouts from Louisiana's Angola ring so strong?
Or, is it because if the truth be told,
You owe me for stealing my people's souls.

Why my History got to be only one month long?

Patti Ross lived in Baltimore, Maryland from 2010 to 2013, just one block south of North Avenue on St. Paul Street. She found herself in a neighborhood somewhat blighted, slighted by its own city. The chess moves of gentrification were becoming more evident and in a short time, Maryland Institute College of Art would move in to change the face of North Avenue between Howard and St. Paul Street forever. Those from the neighborhood saw their displacement coming. They preached about it to whoever would listen and often Patti did.

After retiring from a career in technology, Patti rediscovered her love of writing and shares her voice as the spoken-word artist, little pi. Patti hosts EC Poetry and Prose Open Mic in Ellicott City, Maryland, and the online series First Fridays under the organizational umbrella of Maryland Writers Association of which she is a board member. She also actively supports several Baltimore youth nonprofits as a board member and advisor. A lifelong advocate for the disenfranchised and homeless, Patti writes poems about the racially marginalized as well as society's traumatization of the human spirit. Her poems are published in the *Pen In Hand Journal*, PoetryXHunger website, and Oyster River Pages: *Composite Dreams Issue* as well as other online zines. Follow her blog at littlepisuniverse.com.

About the interior artwork:

Much of my writing stems from my interest in social justice. I come from a family that has always believed the basic right of a human being is to exist at a level of equity in society. My family taught me that it is our responsibility as citizens of this country and members of our communities to work toward inclusion of ALL persons. This nation wrote words in a constitution defining what it means to be a citizen. We must abide by those words. When we say "all men are created equal" it is our duty to put action behind it.

As a writer of poetry and as a spoken-word artist, I hope that my act of creating with both words and speech puts into action a reminder of this: we are all created equal. No man, no woman, is intrinsically better than the next. I hope I shed light on the untold stories of history and the survival of the marginalized people of this country and it's colonization.

I was told once to "write about what haunts you" and when I look over my life, that mantra has been what I have innately followed. My poems and my spoken word are a way of paying reverence to those ancestors that sacrificed their lives for me to live and speak my mind. Through my poetry and spoken work, I hope to speak for them and others that have fear or feel voiceless.

In March 2020, Brianna Taylor would be killed and the realization of a pandemic would settle in. News stories would spin wildly over police and citizens actions, over the wearing of a mask and it's symbolism. What happened to LOVE? What happened to our inner souls? We were in a war with ourselves, our fellow country men, and a virus, and no one was talking about LOVE. So, I started drawing hearts with inner souls.

In the human body, the heart is what keeps the body alive. I believe that what is in the center of the heart is our soul and that determines our social actions. My heart drawings, included here within, usually have a center that depicts a hungriness for change. I draw the same heart shape each time because our heart's are shaped the same but our social action's come from that core center that often haunts us. We have to work to link that center to the belief of LOVE.

Thank you for supporting independent publishing.

Yellow Arrow Publishing is a nonprofit supporting writers that identify as women. Visit YellowArrowPublishing.com for information on our publications, workshops, and writing opportunities.